Get Ahead

Workbook

Janet Hardy-Gould

Nicholas Timms

Great Clarendon Street, Oxford, OX2 6DP, United Kingdom

Oxford University Press is a department of the University of Oxford. It furthers the University's objective of excellence in research, scholarship, and education by publishing worldwide. Oxford is a registered trade mark of Oxford University Press in the UK and in certain other countries

First published in 2013
2017 2016 2015 2014 2013
10 9 8 7 6 5 4 3 2 1

ISBN: 978 0 19 413113 1

Printed in China

This book is printed on paper from certified and well-managed sources

ACKNOWLEDGEMENTS

Illustrations by: Paul Daviz pp.13, 29; Mark Duffin pp.28, 36, 40; Martina Farrow pp.4, 9, 16, 25; Dylan Gibson pp.8, 20, 44; Kev Hopgood pp.49; Chris Pavely pp.12; Martin Sanders pp.43, 48.

The publisher would like to thank the following for permission to reproduce photographs: Alamy Images pp.6 (Teen girl shopping/Asia Images Group Pte Ltd), 26 (Police officer/Marco Secchi), 31 (The Google offices/Duncan Selby); Corbis pp.10 (Footballers/Robert Michael), 27 (Currency exchange counter/ Ocean), 30 (Teen girls/AID/amanaimages), 34 (Teacher with student/Harry Chli/TongRo Images), 45 (Footballer/Catherine Ivill/AMA), 46 (Friends looking at smart phone/Kentaroo Tryman/Maskot), 50 (Teen friends/Kevin Dodge); Getty Images pp.11 (Renho, State Minister/Kazuhiro Nogi/AFP), 33 (Woman using mobile phone/baona), 37 (Leonardo DiCaprio signs autographs/Anne-Christine Poujoulat/AFP); Oxford University Press pp.14 (Cotswolds/Digital Vision), 18 (Doctor and patient/Image Source), 19 (Fruit and vegetables/ Photodisc), 26 (Male using phone/Gareth Boden), 35 (Orangutan with baby/ Eric Gevaert), 38 (Teens shopping/Chris King), 42 (Teen in cafe/Chris King), 51 (Woman portrait/Gareth Boden); Shutterstock pp.5 (Woman in dress/ Gromovataya), 7 (Young man with digital tablet/Dragon Images), 7 (Portrait of woman/RAYphotographer), 15 (Teen portrait/paulaphoto), 15 (Female student/ iodrakon), 22 (Couple walking/merzzie), 23 (Pudding/Sergio Stakhnyk), 43 (Blueberries/matin).

Cover: Getty Images (Traffic light trails/Prachanart); iStockphoto (Airport check-in queue/enviromantic)

Although every effort has been made to trace and contact copyright holders before publication, this has not been possible in some cases. We apologise for any apparent infringement of copyright and, if notified, the publisher will be pleased to rectify any errors or omissions at the earliest possible opportunity.

Contents

1 The look

Vocabulary

Fashion

1 Circle seven words. Then label the picture.

E	A	R	R	I	N	G	S	X	H
S	U	N	G	L	A	S	S	E	S
K	G	F	B	W	H	C	Q	T	H
X	D	V	O	J	B	F	U	S	O
C	A	P	O	Z	E	P	G	H	O
F	P	J	T	H	L	I	K	I	D
Z	C	Q	S	G	T	V	D	R	Y
S	W	E	A	T	P	A	N	T	S

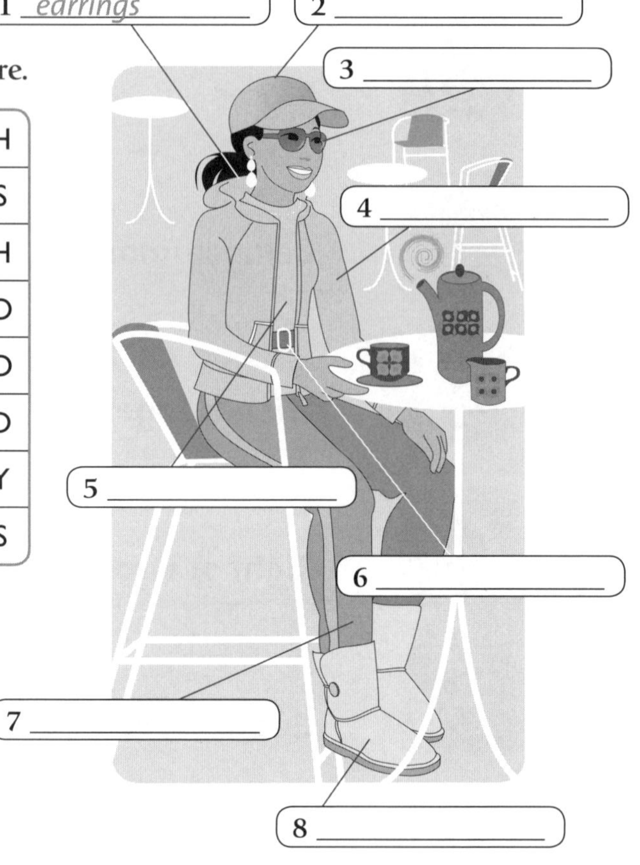

2 Complete the sentences with the words in the box.

earrings high heels leggings sunglasses top ~~vest~~

1 Satoshi always wears a *vest* and jacket to work.
2 I want to buy these small gold ________ for my sister. She loves accessories!
3 Kanya doesn't like wearing jeans. She prefers ________.
4 I always wear my ________ in the summer. It's usually sunny.
5 My friend would like to buy a ________ – perhaps a new T-shirt.
6 Emma is wearing ________ today. She looks very tall!

3 Describe what you are wearing now.

I'm wearing ____

____

____

____

Simple present and present continuous ▪ Tag questions

1 Circle the correct words.

Mia Hi, Ed. What [1] **are you doing / do you do**?
Ed I [2] **'m looking / look** at a magazine.
Mia It's a fashion magazine. You [3] **aren't liking / don't like** fashion!
Ed I know. But we [4] **'re doing / do** a project about fashion.
Mia That's interesting. [5] **Are you needing / Do you need** any help?
Ed Thanks. I [6] **'m looking / look** for photos right now.
Mia I can do that. I [7] **'m loving / love** fashion magazines.
Ed Great! Thanks, Mia.

2 There is a mistake in each sentence. Write the correct words.

1 We're not understanding this article about American fashion. *don't understand*
2 I'm prefering wearing a hoody on weekends. ________
3 Are you liking shopping for clothes? ________
4 What do they do right now? ________
5 My dad doesn't watch TV right now – he's on the phone. ________

3 Complete the sentences with the tag questions from the box.

aren't you	does she	don't you	~~do you~~	isn't she

1 You don't like those big earrings, *do you*?
2 You know that boy in the cap, ________?
3 Your friend is wearing a new top, ________?
4 She doesn't usually buy high heels, ________?
5 You're studying fashion with Jane, ________?

4 Write two sentences about things that are happening now. Then write two sentences about things that happen every day.

I'm doing my English homework now.

____

____

I usually wear a hoody and leggings.

____

____

Clothes shopping

1 Circle the correct words.

Sales clerk	Good morning, can I [1] **help** / **helping** you?
Akira	Yes, thanks. I [2] **'m looking** / **look** for some leggings.
Sales clerk	Well, the leggings are over here … What about [3] **this** / **these** ones?
Akira	Oh, yes! [4] **They're** / **They** very nice, aren't they? Do you have any other colors?
Sales clerk	Yes, they [5] **come** / **comes** in dark green, gray or orange.
Akira	I like the gray ones. Can I [6] **try** / **wear** them on?
Sales clerk	Of course. The [7] **fitting** / **fit** rooms are over there.

2 Put the conversation in the correct order.

Sales clerk	Of course. The fitting rooms are over there.	____
Sales clerk	Hello, can I help you?	1
Sales clerk	Well, the T-shirts are over here … What about this one?	____
Sales clerk	Yes, it comes in light blue, yellow, or red. Red is very nice.	____
May	Oh, yes! It's nice, isn't it? Do you have any other colors?	____
May	Yes, thanks. I'm looking for a T-shirt.	____
May	Yes, I love the red one. Can I try it on?	____

3 Write a new conversation.

Sales clerk	Hello, ________________?
You	Yes, thanks. I'm looking for ________________________________
Sales clerk	____
You	It's very nice, isn't it? ____________________________________
Sales clerk	____
You	I really like ____
	____
Sales clerk	____

Negative prefixes

1 Read the conversations. Complete the adjectives with the correct negative prefix.

1 "I never help my brother with his homework." "You're very _ir_responsible."
2 "Do you always tell the truth?" "Yes. I'm never _____honest!"
3 "Hurry up! We need to leave now!" "Please don't be _____patient."
4 "Are you interested in the latest clothes?" "Not really. I'm very _____fashionable."

2 Read the text. Do you agree with Bo-Han or Sumalee?

MY FASHION STYLE

Bo-Han

I always wear jeans and a T-shirt with sneakers. Boring? Well, to be honest, I'm not really into fashion. And there are some advantages to wearing the same kind of clothes all the time. Firstly, I don't need to think about what to wear. And secondly, people never comment on my clothes which is great, because I don't like people talking about me!

Sumalee

I think fashion is important because your clothes say something about your personality. I'm a confident person and I want my clothes to reflect this. I hate looking unfashionable, even at home! Being fashionable doesn't have to be expensive. I often buy a cheap top and then change it a bit. You don't need a lot of skill – just some imagination! I love it when people comment on my clothes.

3 Read the text again. Circle T (true) or F (false).

1 Bo-Han is very interested in fashion. T F
2 Bo-Han wears different clothes every day. T F
3 Nobody comments on Bo-Han's clothing. T F
4 Sumalee wears unfashionable clothes in her own house. T F
5 Sumalee is happy when people say things about her clothes. T F

4 Answer the questions.

1 What does Bo-Han wear when he goes out with his friends?

____

2 Why is Bo-Han happy that people don't comment on his appearance?

____

3 In Sumalee's opinion, why is fashion important?

____

4 What type of personality does Sumalee have?

____

2 Characters

Vocabulary

Describing personality

1 Complete the sentences with the words in the box.

generous	hard-working	moody	quiet	selfish	~~shy~~

1 She's very _shy_.
2 He's ________.
3 He's very ________.
4 He's a little ________.
5 She's a little ________.
6 She's ________.

2 Circle the correct words.

1 Minjun likes to talk to people. He's **(outgoing)** / **lazy**.
2 My brother is always happy and relaxed. He's **easy-going** / **moody**.
3 You're always happy and smiling. You're a very **serious** / **cheerful** person.
4 Joe often speaks to his friends in class. He's **quiet** / **talkative**.
5 She doesn't laugh very often. She's a very **serious** / **generous** girl.
6 They're **hard-working** / **lazy**. They don't help around the house at all.

3 Complete the sentences about people you know.

1 My teacher's very _cheerful and outgoing_.
2 My brother's / sister's a little ________________.
3 My cousin's very ________________.
4 My best friend isn't ________________, but he's / she's very ________________.
5 My mom isn't very ________________, but she's a little ________________.

Comparative and superlative adjectives ▪ *too … / not … enough*

1 Circle the correct words.

1 Am I (**quieter**) / **quietest** than you?
2 Hong is **more** / **most** easy-going than her cousin.
3 Who's the **moodier** / **moodiest** person in your family?
4 You're always happy. You're the **more** / **most** cheerful person in our school!
5 They are the **lazier** / **laziest** students in our class – they never do their homework.

2 Complete the conversation. Use *too* or *enough* and the words in the box.

generous lazy selfish serious ~~talkative~~

Matt What's the matter, Kathy?
Kathy I'm very angry with my brother, Sam. He says I'm [1] *too talkative* and noisy when we watch his favorite TV program! But when we watch *my* favorite program – he laughs and he isn't [2] ______ about watching it.
Matt Oh dear!
Kathy The problem is that Sam always thinks about himself – he's [3] ______. Also, he isn't [4] ______ with his money! *And* he never helps around the house – he's [5] ______!
Matt He needs to be more like you, Kathy. Perfect!

3 Write comparative and superlative sentences. Use the words in the box and adjectives from exercises 1 and 2.

my friend my sister my brother my mother my family my class my school

1 *I'm more hard-working than my friend Sunisa.*
2 *My brother is the most easy-going person in my family.*
3 ______
4 ______
5 ______
6 ______

Conversation practice

Giving opinions

1 **Put the words in the correct order to make sentences.**

1. the / team / best / He's / on / our / . / player
   He's the best player on our team.
2. my / In / , / too / . / opinion / lazy / Ed's
   ____
3. you / Do / so / ? / think
   ____
4. person / think / I / the / ideal / . / are / you
   ____
5. don't / that / enough / he's / serious / think / . / I
   ____

2 **Circle the correct words.**

David	Who do you want as soccer team captain?
Paul	What about Kevin? He's definitely the [1] **best** / **better** player.
David	He's a great player, but he isn't [2] **lazy** / **serious** enough. What about Ed?
Paul	In my opinion, Ed's [3] **too** / **enough** disorganized.
David	But I think it's more important for a team captain to be [4] **shy** / **confident**.
Paul	Do [5] **I** / **you** think so? Well, you're very confident. Why don't you be our captain?
David	But I'm too busy with my school work for the job!

3 **Write a new conversation between you and a friend about a team captain or class representative.**

Friend	Who do you want as our ______________ this year?
You	What about ______________?
Friend	In my opinion, ______________ ______________.
You	I think it's more important ______________.
Friend	I don't think that ______________ ______________.
You	But ______________.

Compound adjectives

1 **Match the two parts of the phrases.**

1 I listen to people's ideas. I'm open- a haired.
2 Our grandfather is generous. He's kind- b minded.
3 You're never moody. You're not bad- c hearted.
4 Your penfriend isn't fair. He's dark- d shouldered.
5 Tom is a strong man. He's very broad- e tempered.

2 **Read the text. Circle the correct answer.**

The text is about Renhō's …

a likes and interests. b life and personality. c family and children.

A woman in politics

A Renhō is one of the most powerful and well-known women in Japanese politics. She is famous as someone who gives her honest opinions at important meetings.

B She was born in Tokyo to a Japanese mother and a Taiwanese father. As a child, she was smart and hard-working, but she didn't have ambitions to become a politician.

C She studied law at college in Tokyo and graduated in 1990. She worked for a short time as a model, but soon became a TV journalist. Between 1995 and 1997 she studied at Beijing University and she speaks fluent Mandarin Chinese.

D Renhō was first elected as a politician in 2004. She became a government minister in June 2010. Her personality has been strong enough to survive in the male-dominated world of Japanese politics.

E Renhō is a unique politician and we will see more of her in the years to come.

3 **Match the topics 1–5 with the paragraphs A–E.**

1 Her life as a politician. _D_
2 Her future. ______
3 Who she is today. ______
4 Her childhood. ______
5 Her studies and early career. ______

4 **Complete the summary with words from the text.**

Renhō is a [1] _well-known_ Japanese [2] __________. She comes from the city of [3] __________ and she went to [4] __________ there, too. She had different jobs before becoming a politician – she was a [5] __________, and then she worked as a [6] __________. Her first language is Japanese, but she is also fluent in [7] __________. She first entered Japanese politics in [8] __________ and in 2010 she became a minister in the Japanese [9] __________.

3 Places

Vocabulary

Town and countryside

1 Label the pictures with the words in the box.

bridge	~~sidewalk~~	factory	farm	parking garage	woods

1 *sidewalk*

2 ____________

3 ____________

4 ____________

5 ____________

6 ____________

2 Read the definitions and complete the words.

1 A high area of land. h*ill*
2 A place where people drive their cars. h__________
3 A house with only one floor and no upstairs rooms. b__________
4 Water which runs to the ocean. r__________
5 A small town in the country. v__________
6 A large area of water, with land all around it. l__________

3 Look at the picture and complete the paragraph.

I live on the tenth floor of a tall [1] *apartment building* in Kansas City, in the United States. From my bedroom window you can see a [2] __________ where they make cars. My dad works there. You can also see a big [3] __________. It's noisy when the road is busy. If you walk over the [4] __________, you come to green [5] __________, where there are some cows. There's also a [6] __________ where I sometimes go fishing with my brother.

Simple past and past continuous ▪ Adverbs

1 Circle the correct words. Use the simple past and the past continuous.

1 While we **drove** / **were driving** down the highway, we **saw** / **were seeing** an accident.
2 I **didn't listen** / **wasn't listening** when the teacher **called** / **was calling** my name.
3 What **did you do** / **were you doing** when I **called** / **was calling** you?
4 I **fell over** / **was falling over** while I **ran** / **was running** to catch the bus.
5 While they **crossed** / **were crossing** the field, it **began** / **was beginning** to rain.
6 We **were playing** / **played** basketball when we **were losing** / **lost** the ball.

2 Complete the sentences. Use the simple past and the past continuous.

1 We _were walking_ (**walk**) near the lake when we _waved_ (**wave**) to our neighbors.
2 Jim ______________ (**break**) his arm while he ______________ (**play**) soccer.
3 My parents ______________ (**meet**) each other while they ______________ (**work**) in a factory.
4 I ______________ (**not wear**) a coat when I ______________ (**go out**) today.
5 When you ______________ (**arrive**) at school, your friends ______________ (**wait**).
6 I ______________ (**learn**) a lot of English while I ______________ (**stay**) in Oxford.

3 Complete the sentences. Make adverbs from the correct adjective in parentheses.

1 It was sunny and the children were playing _happily_ outside. (**happy** / **sad**)
2 My sister was laughing __________ so we couldn't hear the TV. (**quiet** / **loud**)
3 I was walking __________ because I was very late for school. (**fast** / **slow**)
4 The basketball team played __________ and they lost the game. (**beautiful** / **bad**)
5 The teacher spoke __________ because the students were noisy. (**kind** / **angry**)
6 Joe was working __________, so he was very tired. (**hard** / **good**)

4 Write three true sentences about yesterday. Use the simple past and the past continuous. You can use the phrases in the box to help you.

walk to school	wait for the bus	eat dinner	do homework	watch TV

start to rain	see a friend	hear a knock on the door	cell phone ring

I was walking to school yesterday morning when I saw my friend, Jiwon.

____

____

____

Conversation practice

Describing your vacation

1 **Complete the conversation with the words in the box.**

~~didn't~~	does	wonderful	raining	time
vacation	village	visiting	weather	

Kevin Hi, there, Amy! I [1] *didn't* see you last Friday. Were you on [2] __________?

Amy Yes, I was [3] __________ my aunt.

Kevin Where [4] __________ she live?

Amy In a beautiful [5] __________ near here.

Kevin Did you have a good [6] __________?

Amy Yes, it was [7] __________. We went walking in the hills.

Kevin So, was the [8] __________ nice?

Amy Well, it was [9] __________ when we arrived, but it was sunny later in the week.

2 **Circle the wrong word in each sentence. Then write the correct word.**

1 Hi! I (not) see you last week. Were you on vacation? *didn't*
2 Yes, I was stay with my grandparents. __________
3 Did you having a nice time? __________
4 Yes, it was wonderful. We go walking near a lake. __________
5 Were the weather good? __________
6 Well, it was sunny when we arriving. __________

3 **Look at the conversation in exercise 1. Write a similar conversation about your vacation. Use the ideas in the box to help you.**

awesome	camping	climbing	countryside	friends	mountains

Friend Hi, there! I didn't see you last week. __________?
You __________
Friend __________?
You __________
Friend __________?
You __________
Friend __________?
You __________

Extreme adjectives

1 Read the conversations. Circle the correct words.

1 "It's cold in here!" "Yes, I know. It's **boiling** / **freezing**!"
2 "Did you enjoy your vacation in Australia?" "Yes, thanks. It was **awful** / **wonderful**."
3 "Is that a new bike?" "No, my dad bought it years ago. It's **ancient** / **gorgeous**!"
4 "I'm tired. I walked all around the lake." "Yes, you look **terrifying** / **exhausted**!"
5 "Is your uncle's apartment small?" "No. It's **enormous** / **furious**."

2 Read the texts. Who moved from the city to the country?

Country living *by Emi*

Last summer, we moved to a village because my mom wanted to live near our grandparents. At first, I thought the country was awful and I missed my friends! Fortunately, my grandparents own the local store and I often help them to serve the customers. So I know everybody now! And the best thing of all? We got a dog!

City living *by Mark*

This time last year, I was living in the country. But then we moved to the city, because my father found a new job. At first, I was terrified. I hated the noise and all the people. My new school was enormous with hundreds of students. But after a while I made friends and learned to enjoy city life. There's always an exciting place to go or a new movie to see.

3 Read the texts again. Circle T (true) or F (false).

1	In the beginning, Emi hated the country.	T	F
2	Emi is happy because she has a dog.	T	F
3	Mark liked the city at first.	T	F
4	Mark's new school was very large.	T	F
5	Mark doesn't have any friends in the city.	T	F

4 Answer the questions.

1 Why did Emi move to the country? ______________________
2 Why does Emi know a lot of people in the village? ______________________
3 Where was Mark living a year ago? ______________________
4 Why did Mark move to the city? ______________________
5 What things does Mark like about the city? ______________________

4 Being human

Vocabulary

Illnesses and injuries

1 Complete the crossword puzzle.

1 S	P	R	A	I	N	E	D	A	N	K	L	E
										3 S		
							2 F					
			4 B						A			
5 H							E			T		
6			D									
7 E						E						
										T		

Across

1 I twisted my foot and now I have a _sprained ankle_.

4 Bao can't write in class because he has a __________.

5 My head hurts a lot. I have a terrible __________.

6 We need to buy some more tissues because you have a __________.

7 Please don't play any loud music! I have an __________.

Down

1 I don't want to eat anything right now. I have a __________.

2 Your face looks hot. Do you have a __________?

3 Saki couldn't speak very well yesterday because she had a __________.

2 Circle the correct words.

1 "Did you eat too much food at dinner?" "Yes! And now I have a **cold** / **(stomachache)**."

2 "I felt very hot and cold last night." "Perhaps you had a **fever** / **broken arm**."

3 "Why is your sister walking slowly?" "She has a **sore throat** / **sprained ankle**."

4 "Why weren't you singing?" "Because I have a **sprained ankle** / **sore throat**."

5 "Kosin is holding his forehead." "Yes, I think he has **an earache** / **a headache**."

3 Look at the pictures. Write sentences in your notebook.

Bo has a broken leg and a bad cold.

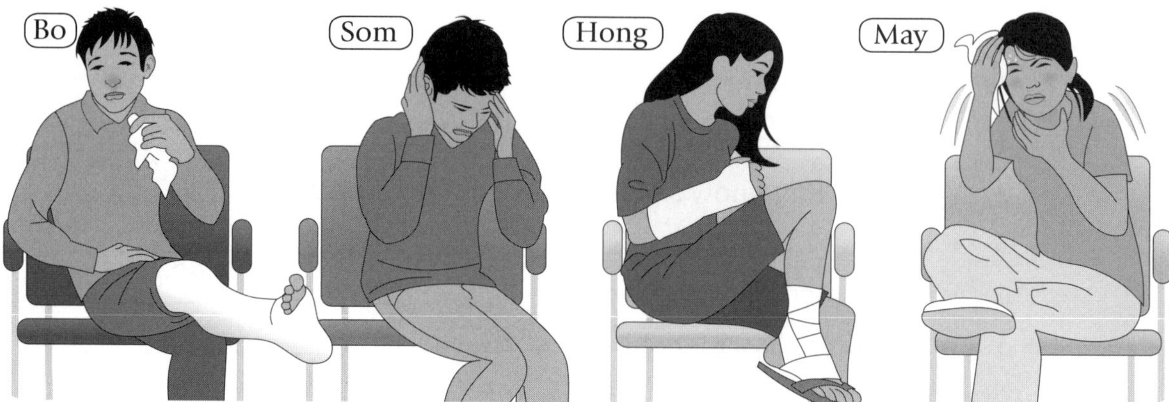

Modal verbs

1 Match the two sentences.

1	You're very late for school!	a	You should take two now.
2	There's a lot of time before the bus comes.	b	You must leave now!
3	That coffee is boiling hot!	c	You don't have to leave now.
4	This tea isn't very hot.	d	You can't drink it right now.
5	These painkillers are good for headaches.	e	You shouldn't take any more.
6	You've taken enough painkillers today.	f	You can drink it now.

2 Complete the conversation. Use *must, must not* or *don't have to* and the verbs in parentheses.

Yu-Ting How often do I need to take these tablets?

Pharmacist You 1 _must take_ (**take**) one tablet every four hours.

Yu-Ting Must I take them with food?

Pharmacist No, you 2 ______________ (**take**) them with food. But you can if you want.

Yu-Ting Is there anything else I need to know?

Pharmacist Yes, you 3 ______________ (**take**) more than eight tablets in 24 hours. That can be dangerous. And you 4 ______________ (**read**) the instructions carefully. Don't forget, if you don't feel well, you 5 ______________ (**go**) to the doctor's immediately.

3 Write advice with *should / shouldn't*.

Your friend …

1 has a bad headache.

You should take some painkillers. You shouldn't go to the party.

2 has an earache.

____

3 is worried about exams.

____

4 would like to have more friends.

____

5 lost his / her cell phone today.

____

6 wants to go abroad in the summer.

____

Conversation practice

At the doctor's

1 Match the two parts of the phrases.

1	What can I do	a	matter?
2	Do you have	b	drink plenty of water.
3	I'm not feeling	c	a day or two.
4	What's the	d	for you today?
5	You should rest for	e	very well.
6	You have to	f	any other symptoms?

2 Put the conversation in the correct order.

Doctor	Do you have any other symptoms?	____
Doctor	What can I do for you today?	1
Doctor	Oh, dear. What's the matter?	____
Doctor	Let me have a look … OK. You should take antibiotics and some painkillers.	____
Doctor	An earache? When did it start?	____
Kim	I have an earache.	____
Kim	On Tuesday evening.	____
Kim	I'm not feeling well today.	____
Kim	Yes, I feel a bit hot.	____

3 Write a conversation at the doctor's. Use the ideas in the box to help you.

cold | drink plenty of water | get some fresh air | headache | stay in bed | stomachache | don't eat too much | take some painkillers

Doctor What can I do for you today?
You ________________
Doctor ________________
You ________________
Doctor ________________
You ________________
Doctor ________________
You ________________
Doctor ________________

Diet and health

1 Match the definitions and the words.

1	How well your body is.	a	weight
2	A person who doesn't eat meat.	b	health
3	How heavy something is.	c	muscles
4	The food that you usually eat.	d	vegetarian
5	These help your body to lift things.	e	calories
6	A plan which can help to make you fitter.	f	diet
7	These show how much energy is in food.	g	exercise program

2 Read Mai's report. Circle the correct answer.

Mai's report is about …

a food shopping. b what her family eats and drinks. c what she eats at school.

My family's diet

I think our diet at home is quite healthy. My parents grow a lot of vegetables so we often eat vegetarian food. We don't usually eat fast food – only if we go to a shopping mall or an amusement park.

Drinks

At home, we usually have fruit juice with our breakfast and we always drink water with our dinner. We sometimes drink tea between meals. I love fizzy drinks, but Mom doesn't buy them often – they have a lot of calories and they're bad for your health.

Possible changes

My family loves eating candy and we often eat chocolate when we're watching a movie at home. We probably shouldn't eat so much candy because it's unhealthy. We should buy more fruit – we could eat that in front of the TV.

3 Answer the questions.

1 What type of food does Mai often eat at home? ______

2 What does Mai drink at dinner time? ______

3 Why doesn't Mai's mother buy fizzy drinks? ______

4 When does Mai's family eat candy? ______

5 What does Mai think they should eat in front of the TV?

______

4 Plan and write three paragraphs about your diet at home. Use the report in exercise 2 to help you.

5 Friends together

Vocabulary

Friendship

1 Look at the pictures. Circle the correct words.

1 **get along** / **have an argument** with somebody

2 **have a falling out with** / **introduce** somebody

3 **have an argument** / **go out** with friends

4 **have a lot in common with** / **introduce** somebody

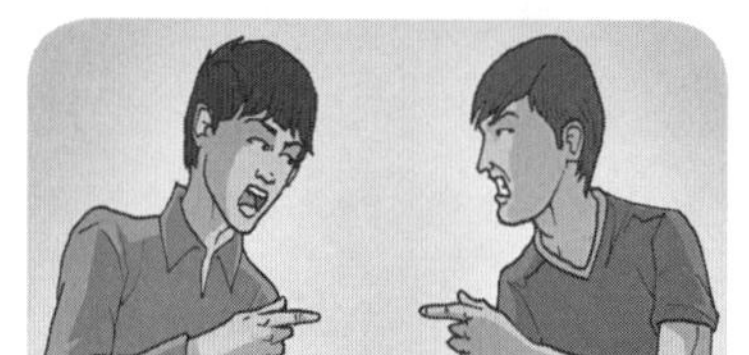

5 **have an argument with** / **get to know** somebody

6 **make up** / **go out** with somebody

2 Complete the conversations with the verbs phrases in the box.

get along get to know go out have a lot in common ~~make friends~~ introduce

1	**Suebin**	I'd like to *make friends* with that new girl.
	Jiwon	I spoke to her yesterday. I can ______________ you to her.
2	**Ya-Wen**	Do you ______________ with your sister?
	Sunisa	Yes. We both love music and cooking so we ______________.
3	**Shota**	I'm planning to ______________ with Kento to that new cafe. His brother's coming, but I don't know him.
	Satoshi	You should talk to his brother and ______________ him.

3 Write about your friendships. Use the phrases from exercises 1 and 2 to help you.

I made friends with Lalita because we have a lot in common.

____

____

Present perfect and simple past ▪ Present perfect with *for* and *since*

1 Circle the correct words.

1 **Did you have** / **Have you had** an argument? You look angry.
2 Yi-Jun **fell out** / **has fallen out** with her best friend yesterday.
3 I'm not coming out with you tonight. I **saw** / **'ve seen** the movie already.
4 **Did they go out** / **Have they been out** with their friends on Saturday?
5 How long **has Dang studied** / **did Dang study** English? He's the best in the class!

2 Complete the phrases with *for* or *since*.

1	*for* fifteen minutes	4	____ six weeks	7	____ four months
2	____ two o'clock	5	____ a short time	8	____ he was ten
3	____ last Friday	6	____ 2010	9	____ 20 minutes

3 Complete the conversation with the present perfect or the simple past.

Bo How long [1] *have you known* (**you** / **know**) Jin?
Hong I [2] ________ (**know**) her for about three years. My friend [3] ________ (**introduce**) me to her at my local tennis club.
Bo How long [4] ________ (**you** / **play**) tennis together?
Hong Jin [5] ________ (**be**) my doubles partner for about two years now.
Bo And when [6] ________ (**play**) your first big tournament together?
Hong Our first important tournament [7] ________ (**be**) at Junior Wimbledon in 2013. I'll never forget it – we won!

4 Write questions with *How long …?* and the present perfect. Then write true answers with *for* or *since*.

1 you / play / the guitar? *How long have you played the guitar?*
I've played the guitar for six years. I've played the guitar since I was eight.
2 your family / live in this town / city? ________
____
____
3 you and your friends / know / each other? ________
____
____
4 your English teacher / teach / at your school? ________
____
____

Conversation practice

Getting to know people

1 Put the words in the correct order to make sentences.

1 you / . / Nice / to / talking *Nice talking to you.*
2 you / again / . / soon / See ______
3 know / me / Let / time / . / next ______
4 before / We've / . / met ______
5 month / Mia's house / We / a / ago / at / . / met ______
6 . / went out / her / last / I / with / week ______

2 Complete the conversation with the phrases from exercise 1.

Ed Hi. You're Jane, aren't you? [1] *We've met before.* I'm Ed.
Jane Yes, I remember. [2] ______
Ed I haven't spoken to Mia for a while. Have you?
Jane Yes, [3] ______. We found a great Thai restaurant.
Ed I love eating Thai food. [4] ______ I'll come too!
Jane Of course!
Ed Thanks. Well, I'd better get back to the library. [5] ______
Jane And you. [6] ______

3 Write a new conversation between you and another person. Imagine that you met each other at a friend's house recently. Use the ideas in the box to help you.

a cafe	the mall	a party	the movies	a friend's house

Friend Hi. You're ______, aren't you? ______
You ______
Friend ______
You ______
Friend ______
You ______
Friend ______
You ______

Compound nouns

1 Match the two parts of the compound nouns.

1	If you want to learn Chinese, you should go to this web	a	friend.
2	Kanya went to the movies yesterday with her new boy	b	site.
3	Our grandmother is never lonely. She has a big family net	c	ache.
4	We can't use our cell phones in the class	d	work.
5	I need to go to bed early. I have a head	e	room.

2 Read the magazine article. Circle the correct answer.

The article is about …

a a cafe in Kyoto. b a factory in Kyoto. c a college convenience store.

Over the last week, social networkers in Kyoto have helped a store in trouble. On Monday morning, 4,000 puddings were delivered to the Kyoto University of Education's store, instead of the usual 20. The mistake came from an error when entering the order onto the system.

At first, selling all of the desserts seemed impossible. But the store workers took a number of steps. They began to sell the puddings at a discount and they put up posters asking students to buy them. They also asked five nearby colleges to buy 3,800 puddings.

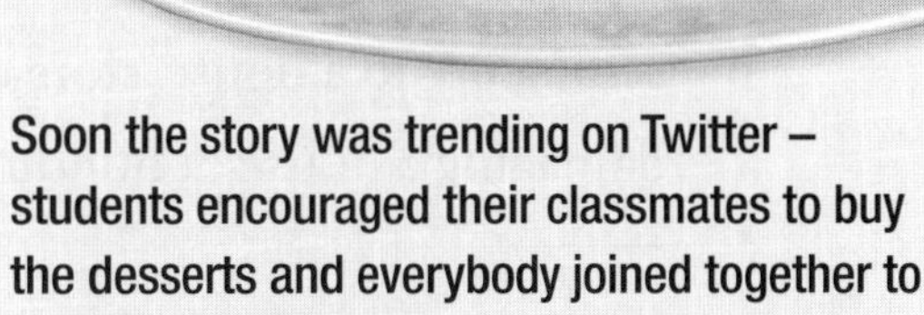

Soon the story was trending on Twitter – students encouraged their classmates to buy the desserts and everybody joined together to help the college store.

The efforts were a success and now all 4,000 puddings have gone. "We are sorry to cause so much trouble," a store worker said.

3 Read the article again. Circle the correct words.

1 The store usually has a delivery of **20** / **3,800** puddings.
2 By mistake, somebody ordered **3,800** / **4,000** puddings.
3 The store did **one thing** / **a number of things** to help with the problem.
4 People put **some** / **a lot of** comments on Twitter.
5 The store asked other **colleges** / **schools** to have some puddings.

4 Answer the questions.

1 Where is the store? ______________________
2 When did the store find it had a problem? ______________________
3 What did the store do to help sell all of the puddings? ______________________
4 What did people on Twitter ask their classmates to do? ______________________

6 Right or wrong?

Vocabulary

Crime

1 **Complete the crossword puzzle.**

Down

1 taking something from a store without paying for it
2 killing someone
5 looking at or changing someone's computer system without asking

Across

2 attacking someone to steal something from them
3 going into someone's house illegally and taking things
4 driving too fast in a car
6 setting fire to a house, store or car
7 damaging a house or building for no good reason

1 SHOPLIFTING

2 **Circle the correct words.**

1 "Someone painted their name on our wall." "**Vandalism** / **Robbery** is a problem."
2 "There was a fire in the shopping mall today." "Do you think it was **hacking** / **arson**?"
3 "Do people steal things from your store?" "No, we don't have a problem with **shoplifting** / **speeding**."
4 "Someone stole money from my bank account." "Was it computer **mugging** / **hacking**?"
5 "People drive too fast here." "Yes, **arson** / **speeding** is very dangerous."

3 **Complete the sentences about crimes. Use your own ideas.**

1 I think ______________ is the worst crime. It's worse than ____________________ because ____.
2 I think __________________ is the most common crime. It's more common than ______________.
3 Vandalism is a problem in cities because ______________________________.
4 The country with the most computer hacking is ______________.
5 I think ______________ is the most dangerous country. There is a lot of ______________ and ______________.

Past perfect

1 **Complete the sentences. Use the past perfect or simple past form of the verbs in the box.**

~~return~~	catch	break	jump	see	not take

1 The robber had left before the family _returned_ home.
2 I remembered that I __________ the murderer somewhere before.
3 She __________ anything from a store before. It was her first crime.
4 We quickly __________ out of bed, but the robber had already disappeared.
5 They had stolen hundreds of cars before the police finally __________ them.
6 He was upset because the vandals __________ all the windows in his car.

2 **Complete the sentences with the past perfect or simple past form of the verbs.**

1 everyone / go / home
The building was very quiet because _everyone had gone home._
2 the police / arrive
The criminals had run away before ____________________.
3 she / forget / her money
She didn't buy anything at the shopping mall because ____________________.
4 I / not enjoy / it
I had seen the movie three times before so ____________________.
5 our friends / already / left
When we arrived at the restaurant ____________________.
6 he / catch / the vandal
The police officer had never caught a criminal before ____________________.

3 **Complete the sentences with the past perfect and your own ideas.**

1 We arrived at the bus stop at 8:15, but the bus _had already left_.
2 The police looked everywhere for the thieves, but they ____________________.
3 Siwon's wallet wasn't in his bag because ____________________.
4 We invited Mai for dinner, but she ____________________.
5 I didn't do well in the exam because ____________________.
6 We invited our friends to see the movie, but they ____________________.

Conversation practice

Reporting a crime

1 Match the two parts of the phrases.

1	Can you	a	anything suspicious?
2	Can you give me	b	broken the window.
3	I'd like to	c	describe what happened?
4	Did you see	d	this exactly?
5	Someone had	e	some more information?
6	Where was	f	report a crime.

2 Circle the correct words.

Amy	My name's Amy Grant. I'd like to report a [1] **crime** / **vandalism**.
Officer	Certainly, Amy. Can you describe what [2] **happened** / **noticed**?
Amy	Yes, I was driving past the shopping mall when I [3] **noticed** / **described** there was paint on the windows of the stores.
Officer	Did you see anyone [4] **reported** / **suspicious**?
Amy	Well, I saw three people running away.
Officer	And where was this [5] **exactly** / **information**?
Amy	On Hill Road. I stopped the car, but I didn't get out.
Officer	Quite right. Can you give me some more [6] **information** / **descriptions**?

3 Write a new conversation. Report one of these crimes.

arson   robbery   mugging   vandalism

You	My name's ______________________
	______________________
Officer	______________________
You	______________________
	______________________
Officer	______________________
You	______________________
Officer	______________________
You	______________________
	______________________
Officer	______________________

Adjective endings

1 **Complete the sentences. Make adjectives from the nouns in the box using *-ful*, *-y*, *-al* and *-ous*.**

anger	care	danger	~~dread~~	fame
	~~guilt~~	mystery	nation	

1 The criminal was *guilty* of a number of *dreadful* murders last year.

2 "Is that man a __________ basketball player?" "Yes, he plays on our __________ team."

3 Nobody understood the robbery at the museum. It was a very __________ crime.

4 The government wants to stop speeding. It can be very __________ to drive too fast.

5 Please be __________ with my laptop. If you break it, I will be very __________.

2 **Read the article. Circle the correct answer.**

The robber left the bank with …

a a lot of money. b a little money. c no money.

The World's Worst Robber

A 58-year-old man went into a branch of a national bank in Tokyo. He didn't have a job, so he decided to rob the bank. But he didn't know what to do. He walked up to an assistant and asked, "Do you know how to rob a bank?"

The assistant asked the man to wait and then quickly spoke to another member of staff. They called the police, then the assistant calmly asked the man to leave and began to walk with him to the door.

However, as she was taking the man out of the bank she noticed a knife in his pocket and some blood on his pants. The bank robber had injured himself earlier with his own knife.

The police immediately arrested the man for carrying a dangerous weapon.

The full story soon appeared in the local newspaper and on TV. Everybody learned how he had asked about robbing the bank, how he had injured himself and how he had left without any money! He truly was the world's worst bank robber!

3 **Read the article again. Put the sentences in the correct order.**

a The police arrested the man. The story was in the media. ____

b As they were walking to the door, the assistant saw the man had a knife. ____

c The man came into the bank. *1*

d The assistant asked the man to leave. ____

e The man asked the assistant how to rob a bank. ____

f The assistant called the police. ____

4 **Answer the question. Why was the man the "world's worst bank robber?"**

7 Get to work!

Vocabulary

Jobs

1 Complete the job adverts with the words in the box. There are two extra jobs.

accountant	construction worker	~~desk clerk~~	doorman
engineer	nurse	office worker	surgeon

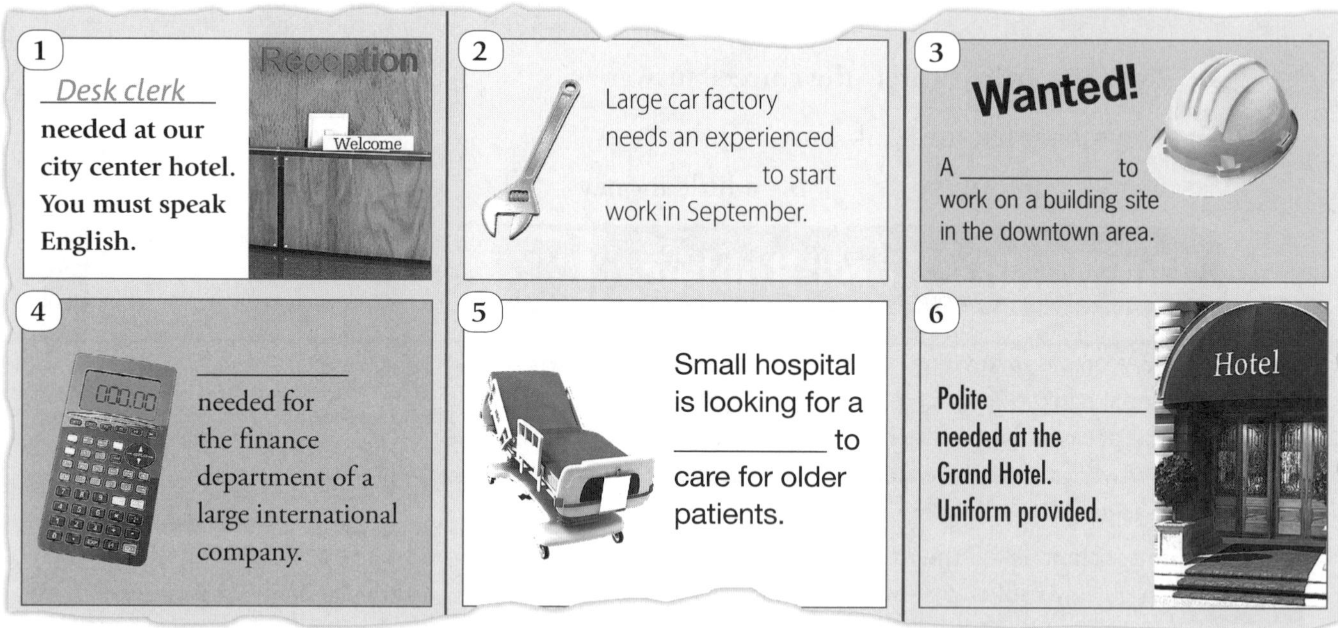

2 Complete the sentences with the words in the box.

badly paid	boring	challenging	~~physical~~

1 Construction workers often need to lift heavy things. It's a very *physical* job.
2 "Is your job rewarding?" "No, it's ________! I do the same thing every day."
3 Suebin has a ________ office job. She doesn't earn much money.
4 Surgeons have a very difficult job. It can be ________ and stressful work.

3 Write sentences about the jobs of people you know. Use words from exercises 1 and 2 to help you.

My neighbor is a teacher. His job is responsible and satisfying.

____

____

____

so / such ▪ *not as ... as*

1 **Put the words in the correct order to make sentences.**

1 job / as / isn't / . / satisfying / My / yours / as
My job isn't as satisfying as yours.

2 early / get up / as / her / as / husband/ . / doesn't / She
____

3 as / isn't / you / hard-working / as / . / Peter
____

4 aren't / Doormen / . / well paid / engineers / as / as
____

5 work / I / as / . / friend / hard / as / my / don't
____

2 **Look at the pictures. Complete the sentences with *not as … as*.**

1 Emi *isn't as tall as Saki*. **(tall)**
2 Today __________ yesterday. **(sunny)**
3 My dog __________ your dog. **(fat)**
4 Matt __________ Ed. **(fit)**

3 **Complete the sentences with *so* or *such* and a word from the box.**

laughed	~~leave~~	tired	asleep	late

1 He has *such* a stressful job that he's going to *leave*.
2 My work is __________ satisfying that I usually stay __________.
3 Her job is __________ boring that she often falls __________ at her desk.
4 We work __________ long hours that we always feel __________ in the evenings.
5 The movie was __________ funny that I __________ the whole time.

4 **Complete the sentences with *so* or *such* and your own ideas.**

1 I have *such* a rewarding job that *I often work long hours*.
2 The movie was __________ scary that ______________________________.
3 It was __________ a sunny day that ______________________________.
4 We are __________ excited about our vacation that ______________________________.

Conversation practice

Comparing and contrasting

1 **Match the two parts of the phrases.**

1	That's such	a	cold in Canada!
2	But it's so	b	as the US.
3	Singapore isn't as expensive	c	long as the one here.
4	And it's closer	d	a great idea!
5	The course doesn't take as	e	to home.

2 **Complete the conversation with the phrases from exercise 1.**

Lalita What are you looking at, Mai?

Mai I'm reading about English courses in Singapore. I need a good qualification in English because I want to study International Business.

Lalita 1 *That's such a great idea*, Mai!
2 ____________________

Mai Exactly. It's a bit cheaper. 3 ____________________.
What do you plan to study next year?

Lalita I'm interested in doing an accountancy course. I'd like to go to Canada, if I can. 4 ____________________

Mai 5 ____________________

Lalita I know! But I'm going to buy some warm clothes so I'll be OK.

Mai That's good.

3 **Write a conversation with a friend comparing and contrasting two things. Choose one of the ideas in the box or use your own idea.**

Which college?	What language to learn?	Where to go on vacation?

You *What are you doing?*
Friend ____________________
You ____________________
Friend ____________________
You ____________________
Friend ____________________
You ____________________
Friend ____________________

Verbs and adjectives + prepositions

1 Complete the sentences. Use the verbs in the box in the correct form and the prepositions *in, on, for* or *about*.

apply	depend	interest	~~worry~~

1 Kosin and Kanya's jobs are well paid. They don't need to *worry about* money.
2 I'm ______________ a career in I.T.
3 We're planning to ______________ jobs in the US next year.
4 "Are you going to college?" "It ______________ my exam results."

2 Read the article. Circle the correct answer.

Working at Googleplex is … **a** challenging but varied. **b** responsible and stressful.

Googleplex

Google is one of the most successful companies in the world. People call the company's main offices in California "Googleplex." They aren't like most other offices. Although the employees work hard, there is also time for play. The company provides swimming pools and a gym. There are also table tennis tables and pinball machines.

Hungry? There are eleven different cafes at Googleplex and the food is all free. Tired? Employees can go to sleep on one of the large, comfortable sofas.

At Google, employees wear jeans, T-shirts and occasionally pyjama pants. Employees with children can bring them into the offices. Even employees' dogs are welcome!

Google began in the 1990s, and at first there were only seven employees. Today, the company employs more than 10,000 people around the world. In fact, the company is so popular that somebody applies for a job every 25 seconds.

3 Complete the sentences with words or numbers from the text.

1 Google's main offices are often called ______________.
2 At Googleplex, people work hard but they can __________, too.
3 You don't need to pay for the __________ at Googleplex.
4 Employees can wear __________ at Googleplex.
5 Now, Google has more than __________ employees.

4 Answer the questions.

1 Where is Googleplex? ______________________
2 What activities does the company have? ______________________
3 What can workers do when they feel tired? ______________________
4 How often does someone apply for a job? ______________________

8 Fragile Earth

Vocabulary

Environmental problems

1 **Find words to complete the sentences.**

1 People think the Earth is getting hotter because of global *warming*.
2 Tigers are an example of an endangered __________.
3 Many animals have now lost their natural __________.
4 Coal and oil are types of fossil __________.
5 Some countries might have less rain in the future because of climate __________.
6 Wind power is an important type of renewable __________.
7 When we burn coal and oil they release carbon __________.
8 Some places may soon be under water because of rising sea __________.

W	A	R	M	I	N	G	P	S
B	D	I	O	X	I	D	E	P
E	Z	C	N	Y	L	K	C	E
N	K	H	U	Z	E	D	F	C
E	J	A	I	J	V	W	U	I
R	T	N	P	V	E	T	E	E
G	D	G	S	Z	L	J	L	S
Y	U	E	Y	W	S	T	S	V
N	Z	H	A	B	I	T	A	T

2 **Complete the definitions with the words in the box.**

carbon dioxide | carbon emissions | climate change | endangered species | renewable energy | ~~solar power~~

1 When you use the sun to make hot water, etc. *solar power*
2 A gas which people often call CO_2. __________
3 Animals or plants that might disappear from the Earth one day. __________
4 Gases which come from using fuels like oil or coal. __________
5 A permanent change in the weather. __________
6 When we use the sun, sea or wind to make power. __________

3 **What are people doing about global warming in your country?**

1 *The government is asking factories to reduce their carbon emissions.*
2 My school __________.
3 My family __________.
4 My friends __________.
5 I __________.

will / be going to

1 Circle the correct words.

1 "I've lost my cell phone." "I **'ll** / **'m going to** lend you mine."
2 What time **will the movie / is the movie going to** start?
3 We've booked our vacation. We **'ll / 're going to** go to Thailand.
4 "Can you keep a secret?" "Yes, I **won't / 'm not going to** tell anyone."
5 I can hear the train now. It **'ll / 's going to** arrive very soon.
6 Do you think jobs **will / are going to** be as well paid in the future?

2 Complete the phone conversation. Use *will* or *be going to* and the verbs in parentheses.

Dad Hi, Kim. Where are you?
Kim Hi, Dad. I'm at the climate-change meeting in town.
Dad What time [1] _are you going to come_ (you / come) home?
Kim I don't know. I think the meeting [2] ______________ (finish) at about five.
Dad How are you going to get home? [3] ______________ (you / catch) the bus?
Kim No. I don't have any money. And it's dark and cloudy outside, so I think [4] ______________ (it / rain) …
Dad OK, I [5] ______________ (give) you a lift.
Kim I [6] ______________ (meet) you outside the library. Thanks, Dad!
Dad No problem. I [7] ______________ (see) you there at 5:30. Bye.

3 Complete the sentences. Use *will* or *be going to* and your own ideas.

1 _In the future, everybody will use renewable energy._
2 I predict that in ten years the environment ______________________________.
3 We have plans for this weekend. We ______________________________.
4 My friends have decided that tomorrow they ______________________________.
5 I have promised my parents that I ______________________________.
6 Look! That boy is going too fast on his bike. He ______________________________.

Conversation practice

Making arrangements

1 Put the words in the correct order to make sentences.

1 . / great / be / That'll — *That'll be great.*
2 call / I'll / later / . / you — ______
3 make / going / . / dinner / to / Emi / for / I'm — ______
4 you / plans / Do / Saturday / have / for / ? / any — ______
5 wait / . / you / hear / I'll / to / from — ______
6 want / time / meet / ? / What / do / you / to — ______

2 Complete the conversation with phrases from exercise 1.

Sara [1] *Do you have any plans for Saturday?*
Kim [2] ______ It's her birthday.
Sara Oh, I'll help, if you like.
Kim Will you? [3] ______ Ken and Lisa are going to come, too.
Sara That's good. It won't take long with four of us.
Kim Let's all meet at my apartment on Saturday.
Sara OK. [4] ______?
Kim I'll talk to my dad and [5] ______
Sara Thanks. [6] ______

3 Write a conversation. Make arrangements to do something with a friend. Use the ideas in the box to help you.

plan a trip | write a brochure for a campaign | work on a school project

Friend Do you have any plans for the weekend?
You ______
Friend ______
You ______
Friend ______
You ______
Friend ______
You ______
Friend ______

Adjectives ending in *-ing* and *-ed*

1 **Complete the conversations. Use the *-ing* or *-ed* form of the words in the box.**

confuse	disappoint	fascinate	~~irritate~~	worry

1 "Does your little sister annoy you?" "Yes, she's really *irritating* sometimes."
2 "Was that talk about the rainforest interesting?" "Yes, it was ____________."
3 "I worked hard for that exam, but I didn't pass." "You must feel ____________."
4 "Did you understand that book?" "No. I thought the story was very ____________."
5 "I'm __________ about global warming." "Yes, I agree. It's very alarming."

2 **Read the text. Circle the correct answer.**

This text is from …

a a magazine about pets. b an environmental campaign brochure.

Save the **orangutan**

Orangutans once lived in a large area from southern China to the foothills of the Himalayas and south to Java. Now, this endangered species only survives on the islands of Borneo and Sumatra.

A century ago, there were about 230,000 orangutans in Borneo and Sumatra. But in the last decade, there has been an alarming fall in their numbers of between 30 and 50%. Now only about 7,500 survive on Sumatra and 55,000 on Borneo.

Threats

The most worrying threat to orangutans is the destruction of their natural habitat. In the last 20 years, around 80% of the orangutan habitat has disappeared and it will continue to disappear in the future. Despite legal protection in Sumatra and Borneo, orangutans are often killed for their meat or caught for the pet trade.

How are you going to help?

You can help orangutans by:
- donating money to protection organizations in Borneo
- adopting a baby orangutan online.

3 **Read the text again. Circle the correct words.**

1 Now, orangutans only live on **two** / **four** islands.
2 There were 230,000 orangutans in Borneo and Sumatra **100** / **ten** years ago.
3 In the last ten years, the number of orangutans has dropped **slowly** / **suddenly**.
4 **Climate change** / **Habitat destruction** is a big problem for the orangutan.
5 According to the text, you can help orangutans in **two** / **three** different ways.

4 **Write a brochure about an endangered animal in your country. Check your work carefully for spelling, punctuation, grammar and vocabulary.**

9 Money, money, money

Vocabulary

Money

1 Look at the pictures and write the words.

ATM cash cash register change ~~PIN number~~ price receipt reduced

1 *PIN number*
2 ____________
3 ____________
4 ____________
5 ____________
6 ____________
7 ____________
8 ____________

2 Circle and write the correct words.

1 "How much is that book?" "The *price* is on the back."
 a receipt b PIN number (c) price
2 "How much is this plastic bag?" "It's __________."
 a reduced b free c cash
3 "Did you exchange your camera?" "No, the store gave me a __________."
 a refund b receipt c price
4 "Please check the price and enter your __________."
 a PIN number b change c ATM
5 "Were those shoes expensive?" "No, they were reduced in the __________."
 a refund b ATM c sale

3 Complete the sentences. Use words from exercises 1 and 2 and your own ideas.

1 My mother *often buys clothes in the end-of-season sale.*
2 My favorite store is ______________ because ______________________.
3 The last time I asked for a refund was ______________________.
4 It's a good idea to keep receipts so that ______________________.

Second conditional

1 **Circle the correct words.**

1 If I **had** / **'d have** a lot of money, I **bought** / **'d buy** a laptop.
2 It **was** / **would be** fantastic if we **won** / **'d win** the lottery.
3 If you **were** / **would be** rich, you **gave** / **'d give** money to charity.
4 If he **check** / **checked** his change, he **saw** / **'d see** the mistake.
5 She **didn't walk** / **wouldn't walk** to school if she **'d own** / **owned** a bike.
6 What would they **watch** / **watched** if they **'d have** / **had** a DVD player?
7 I would tell my parents if I **was** / **'d be** upset.

2 **Complete the sentences using the correct form of the verbs.**

1 see / buy
If she _saw_ that top in the sale, she _'d buy_ it.
2 not go / be
I ______________ near that big dog if I ______________ you!
3 (you) be / forget
______________ upset if your best friend ______________ your birthday?
4 lose / not be able to
If he ______________ his keys, he ______________ get into the house.
5 not get up / not have to
They ______________ early if they ______________ go to school.
6 travel / have
We ______________ around the world if we ______________ enough money.

3 **Write second conditional sentences. Use the phrases in the box or your own ideas.**

meet my favorite movie star	see the US president
live in Sydney	find someone's passport
work in a chocolate factory	be very good at soccer
lose my camera	have a fast car

1 _It would be fantastic if I met my favorite movie star._
2 ______________________________
3 ______________________________
4 ______________________________
5 ______________________________
6 ______________________________

Talking about imaginary situations

1 Circle the correct words.

1 Did you hear the **news** / **incredible**?
2 Really? That's **kidding** / **incredible**!
3 If that **imagined** / **happened** to me, I'd spend the money on clothes.
4 No, I didn't. **Where** / **What** happened?
5 You're **wow** / **kidding**!

2 Put the conversation in the correct order.

Dan	A girl found a $10,000 diamond necklace on the bus.	___
Dan	I'm not sure, but can you imagine if that happened to you?	___
Dan	Did you see the news on TV last night?	1
Dan	You're kidding! I'd give it to the police. It would be wrong to keep it.	___
Anna	Really? That's incredible! Can she keep it?	___
Anna	Wow! If that happened to me, I'd keep it and wear it to school.	___
Anna	No, I didn't. What happened?	___

3 Write a conversation about something surprising in the news. Use the ideas in the box to help you.

saw a lion in the street | bought a Picasso for $100
man fell 4000 m and wasn't injured | 80-year-old climbed Everest

You Did you hear the news?
Friend ______________________________
You ______________________________
____
Friend ______________________________
You ______________________________
____
Friend ______________________________
____
You ______________________________

Money: phrasal verbs

1 Match the two parts of the phrases.

1	I borrowed some money from Shota. I'll pay	a	for a refund.
2	If the sunglasses are broken, you should ask	b	him back.
3	Chi doesn't have a lot of money so she shops	c	up for a new computer.
4	I didn't like the jacket so I took it	d	around for the best price.
5	Can you pay for the groceries? I've run	e	back to the store.
6	Trang is saving	f	out of money.

2 Read the text. Who bought the car? Circle the correct answer.

a George Foster b Harriet Foster c Eve Foster

Mom, I bought a car!

Last week George Foster got an e-mail from eBay. The message said, "Congratulations! The car is now yours! Please pay immediately." George was surprised.

"I couldn't understand it," he said. "I asked Harriet, my wife, but she knew nothing about it." According to the website, he had bought a 1961 pink Cadillac.

They were about to ring the car owner when Eve, their three-year-old daughter announced, "Mom! Dad! I bought a pink car on the computer!"

Harriet thinks she left her eBay password on her laptop. "I think Eve just pressed all the right keys," said Harriet. "I shouldn't keep my password on the computer, but if I didn't keep it there, I'd never remember it!"

George rang the owner Keith Masters. "Luckily, he thought it was amusing," said George.

"We need to save up for a while before we start buying Cadillacs," laughed George.

3 Read the text again. Circle T (true) or F (false).

1	George's wife knew all about the car.	T	F
2	The car on eBay was an old Cadillac.	T	F
3	Eve is a teenager.	T	F
4	Eve used her mother's password.	T	F
5	The owner wanted George to pay for the car.	T	F

4 Answer the questions.

1 How did Eve's parents find out what she had done? ____________________

2 What color was the car? ____________________

3 Why does Harriet keep her password on her laptop? ____________________

4 What did Keith Masters think about the situation? ____________________

5 Why can't George buy the car? ____________________

10 On the menu

Vocabulary

Typical dishes

1 These words don't match the pictures. Write the correct words.

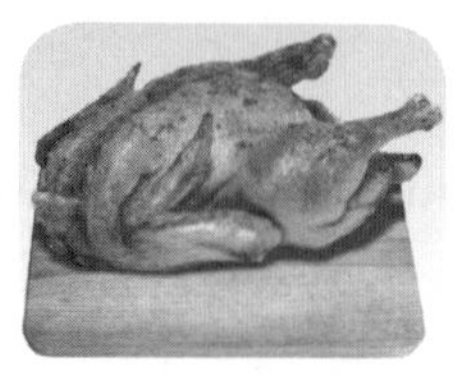

1 ~~tomatoes~~ *olives*	2 green beans ______	3 sausage ______	4 mushrooms ______	5 carrots ______

6 potatoes ______	7 olives ______	8 beansprouts ______	9 bell pepper ______	10 chicken ______

2 Complete the definitions with the correct word.

beef cheese gravy noodles olives ~~tomatoes~~

1 People often think that these are vegetables, but they're actually fruit. *tomatoes*
2 You can put this brown sauce over meat and vegetables. ______
3 These are long and thin – they're made from rice or wheat. ______
4 This meat comes from a cow. ______
5 You can eat these green or black fruits or make them into oil. ______
6 This is white or yellow. Two different types are cheddar and mozzarella. ______

3 Complete the sentences. Use your own ideas.

1 My mom makes *a wonderful dish with chicken, mushrooms and noodles.*
2 I can cook ______.
3 My favorite dish from my country is ______.
4 My favorite dish from another country is ______.
5 In my family, we eat a lot of ______.
6 In my family, we don't eat ______.

The passive

1 Circle the correct words.

1 All of our vegetables are **grew** / **grown** in the garden.
2 These olives **isn't** / **aren't** sold in supermarkets.
3 Were these noodles **made** / **make** in China?
4 All of these ingredients **was** / **were** bought yesterday. They're really fresh.
5 This cheese **wasn't** / **weren't** imported from abroad. It was made here.

2 **Write questions using the present or past passive. Then choose the correct word and write answers.**

1 Where / most of the world's coffee / produce ? **a** Germany **b** Brazil
Where is most of the world's coffee produced?
Most of the world's coffee is produced in Brazil.

2 Where / the dish Kimchi / eat ? **a** Korea **b** Japan
______
______

3 In which country / most of the world's bananas / grow ? **a** the UK **b** India
______
______

4 In which city / the first pizzas / make ? **a** London **b** Naples
______
______

5 Where / the first potatoes / discover ? **a** South America **b** Australia
______
______

3 **Write four passive sentences about food. Use the words in the box to help you.**

the best	the most delicious	the cheapest	the first

find	grow	import from	make	produce	sell

The best sushi in the world is made by my grandmother!
The first Italian food was sold in our country in the 1960s.
______
______
______
______

Conversation practice

In a restaurant

1 Match the two parts of the phrases.

1	Are you ready	a	sugar, salt and oyster extract.
2	What's that	b	or drinks?
3	What would	c	to order?
4	Any side orders	d	made with?
5	It's made with	e	what this one is?
6	Could you tell me	f	you like with that?

2 Complete the conversation with the phrases from exercise 1.

Waiter Hello there. 1 *Are you ready to order* ?
Anna Not yet. 2 ________________________?
Waiter Beef chow mein? That's beef, noodles and vegetables in an oyster sauce.
Anna Oyster sauce? 3 ________________________? Is it spicy?
Waiter No, it isn't. 4 ________________________
Anna Thank you. That sounds very good. I'll try it.
Waiter 5 ________________________?
Anna Sweet and sour vegetables, please.
Waiter Of course. 6 ________________________?
Anna I think I'll have a glass of water, please.

3 Choose your favorite type of restaurant. Write a conversation with a waiter.

Waiter *Are you ready to order?*
You ________________________
Waiter ________________________
You ________________________
Waiter ________________________
You ________________________
Waiter ________________________
You ________________________
Waiter ________________________
You ________________________

Quantities

1 Look at the picture. Which phrases are correct? Change the incorrect phrases.

1 ☒ a box of cereal *a bowl of cereal*
2 ☐ a cup of orange juice ________
3 ☐ a piece of noodles ________
4 ☐ a slice of cake ________
5 ☐ a bottle of lemonade ________

2 Read the magazine article. Which three foods are *superfoods*?

Superfoods

All foods have some nutritional value. However, some foods are so good for you that they're known as "superfoods."

All fish is high in protein and vitamins. But **oily** fish, like salmon, is very good for you. If you eat salmon, you're less likely to have heart problems. What's more, fish keeps your brain healthy!

The fat in olive oil is also good for your heart. However, olive oil has lots of **calories**, so it gives you energy, but can make you put on weight.

Blueberries contain antioxidants. These are chemicals that can protect you against **cancer**. However, blueberries are often imported by airplane into countries like Japan. So blueberries are good for you, but they are bad for the environment!

Although "superfoods" are healthy, it's important to eat lots of different foods. "A bowl of blueberries isn't enough to make you healthy," says **nutritionist** Lucy Turnbull.

Blueberries contain antioxidants

3 Match the words and the definitions.

1 oily — a the amount of energy a food contains
2 calories — b a person who knows a lot about food and nutrition
3 cancer — c containing a lot of oil
4 nutritionist — d a serious disease

4 Complete the summary with words from the text.

Superfoods are foods that are very [1] *good* for you. One example is oily fish, like [2] ________. It is good for your [3] ________ and your [4] ________. [5] ________ is another superfood which is good for your heart, but it contains a lot of [6] ________.

[7] ________ are another example of a superfood. They contain lots of [8] ________, which protect your body against [9] ________.

11 Invention

Vocabulary

Mechanisms

1 Complete the crossword puzzle.

Across

2 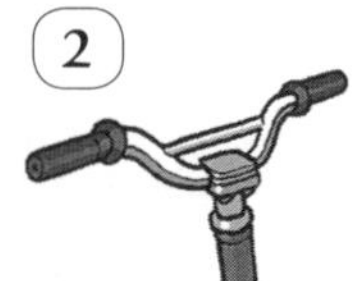
5 
6 

10
11 
12 

Down

1 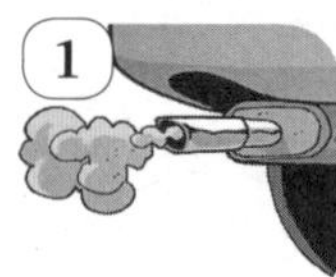
3 

4 
7 
8 
9 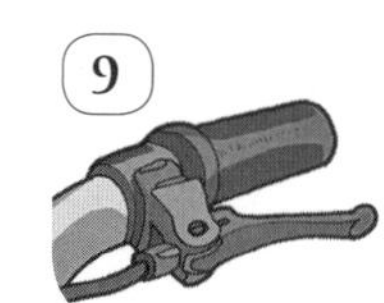

2 Complete the definitions with a word from Exercise 1.

1 You press this to stop or start electricity. _switch_
2 The waste gases from a car come out of this. ________
3 This turns round fast and makes a helicopter move. ________
4 You use these to slow down or stop. ________
5 A car has four; a bike has two; they are round. ________
6 You put your hands on these when you're riding a bike. ________

3 Complete the sentences with your own ideas.

1 Some of the early cars had _small engines and only three gears._
2 Most modern cars now have ________________.
3 One day, I'd like to buy a car with ________________.
4 The best type of bikes have ________________.
5 My bike has ________________.
6 In the past, a lot of planes had ________________.

Relative clauses

1 **Complete the sentences with *who, which* or *where*.**

1 This is the new factory _where_ all the control panels are made.
2 Frank Whittle was the man ________ invented the turbojet engine.
3 Can you show me a bike ________ has the new type of brakes?
4 This is the city ________ the famous scientist was born.
5 Are you the person ________ sold me the car?
6 Here's the pedal ________ is broken.

2 **Rewrite the sentences with *who, which* or *where*.**

1 I'll show you the store. I bought my smartphone there.
I'll show you the store where I bought my smartphone.
2 The engineer has invented a new tail pipe. It reduces carbon emissions.
____
3 We're going to call the man. He can repair your wheel.
____
4 They went to the museum. You can see old propeller planes there.
____
5 She's bought a fantastic mountain bike. It has twenty gears.
____
6 What was the name of the woman? She discovered radium.
____

3 **Complete the sentences using relative pronouns and your own ideas.**

1 Park Ji-Sung is a soccer player
who has played for two different British teams.
2 The Smart Car is a car
________________.
3 Thailand is a country
________________.
4 Leonardo DiCaprio is an actor
________________.
5 Okinawa is an island
________________.
6 You can buy tablet computers
________________.

Conversation practice

Explaining how things work

1 Put the words in the correct order to make sentences.

1 problem / ? / What's / the *What's the problem?*

2 a / press / which / button / here / you / . / There's

____

3 hand / , / you / please / Could / ? / me / give / a

____

4 working / . / camera / My / isn't / new

____

5 camera / the / is / which / the / . / This / turns on / button

____

2 Circle the correct words.

Yan-Ting	Hi, Shi-Han! Could you give me a [1] **hand** / **help**, please? My new camera isn't [2] **working** / **work**.
Shi-Han	Yes, of course. What's the [3] **problem** / **wrong**?
Yan-Ting	This is the button which [4] **turns** / **presses** on the camera, isn't it?
Shi-Han	I think so.
Yan-Ting	But when I press it, [5] **not** / **nothing** happens. It's very annoying!
Shi-Han	Let me see. Oh, I know. You're pressing the wrong button. That's the zoom.
Yan-Ting	Really?
Shi-Han	Yes, there's a button [6] **which** / **where** you press here. Can you see?
Yan-Ting	Oh, right. Thank you.

3 Write a new conversation between you and a friend. Write about a problem with an object from the box.

smartphone laptop MP3 player watch remote-controlled car

You	Hi! Could you ______________________________?
Friend	______________________________
You	______________________________
Friend	______________________________
You	______________________________
Friend	______________________________
You	______________________________
Friend	______________________________
You	______________________________

Vocabulary and reading

Materials

1 Complete the sentences with the correct words.

1 Those cups won't break. They're made of _aluminum_. (**leather / china / aluminum**)
2 This beautiful dress is made of Chinese __________. (**silk / steel / rubber**)
3 Be careful with those __________ plates! (**plastic / rubber / china**)
4 "Is that a __________ sweater?" "Yes, it is. It's very warm!" (**brick / wool / bamboo**)
5 Here's the new skyscraper which is made of __________ and glass. (**steel / nylon / gold**)

2 Read the text. Circle the correct answer.

The article is about environmentally-friendly …

a transport. **b** homes. **c** technology.

New inventions

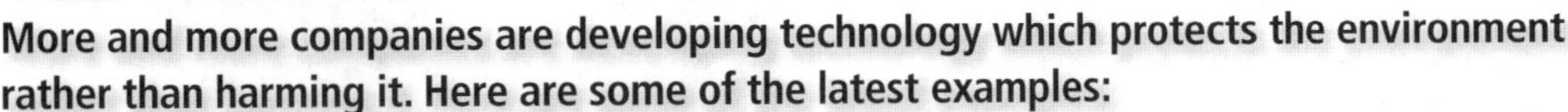

More and more companies are developing technology which protects the environment rather than harming it. Here are some of the latest examples:

Power walking

Every step that you take uses energy. What happens to that energy? Usually, it is wasted. But an American company called PowerLeap is trying to change that. They have invented a new kind of floor which generates electricity from people's footsteps. In a normal home, it would not make a big difference. But in a place where there are large numbers of people, for example, a railway station, it could make a lot of electricity.

Green machine

Most washing machines use a lot of water and energy. However, a British company is developing a machine which washes clothes without water! The dirt is removed by thousands of small balls of plastic. The clothes come out of the machine dry – so a dryer isn't needed. This technology could reduce the world's water and energy use. If every home in the world used one, CO_2 emissions would fall by 28 million tons a year!

3 Circle the wrong word in each sentence. Then write the correct word.

1 The PowerLeap company has made a new type of (energy). __________
2 The new floor can make a lot of energy in a family home. __________
3 The inventors of the new washing machine work in the US. __________
4 When the clothes leave the washing machine they are wet. __________

4 Answer the questions.

1 How is electricity generated from the floor? __________
2 Where could people make a lot of electricity? __________
3 Why are washing machines bad for the environment? __________
4 Which invention do you think is the best? Why? __________

____

12 Communicate

Vocabulary

The Internet

1 Find and write seven words.

L	I	N	K	C	J	M	F
I	V	U	Z	L	X	E	D
C	D	A	F	I	K	N	T
A	X	P	W	P	Q	U	R
N	F	O	L	D	E	R	A
T	O	O	L	B	A	R	S
I	N	B	O	X	Z	Y	H
V	Y	C	U	R	S	O	R

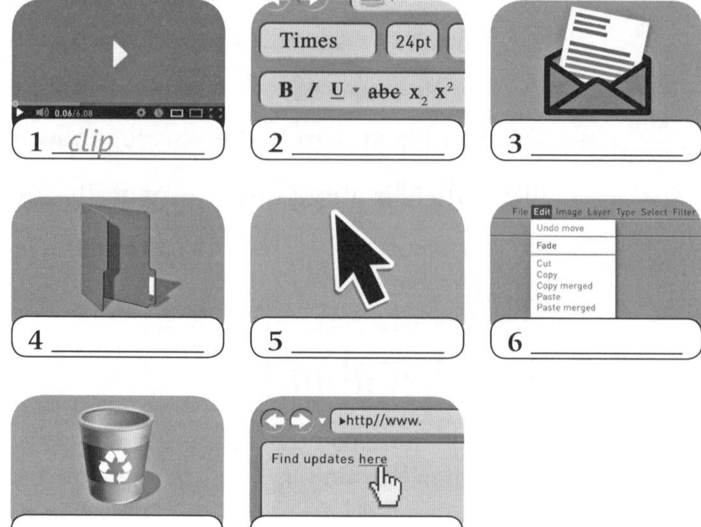

1 *clip*
2 ______
3 ______
4 ______
5 ______
6 ______
7 ______
8 ______

2 Circle the correct words.

1 When Jun turned on his laptop, he found 100 e-mails in his **icon** / **inbox**.
2 To go to the correct website, type the address in your web **menu** / **browser**.
3 The government wants to improve the **broadband** / **document** speed in this area.
4 If you need to work on two things at once, you open a new **window** / **cursor**.
5 Suemin used the **folder** / **search engine** to find websites about studying in the US.
6 I've sent you the information by e-mail. The **menu** / **document** is attached.

3 Write definitions for the words and phrases below.

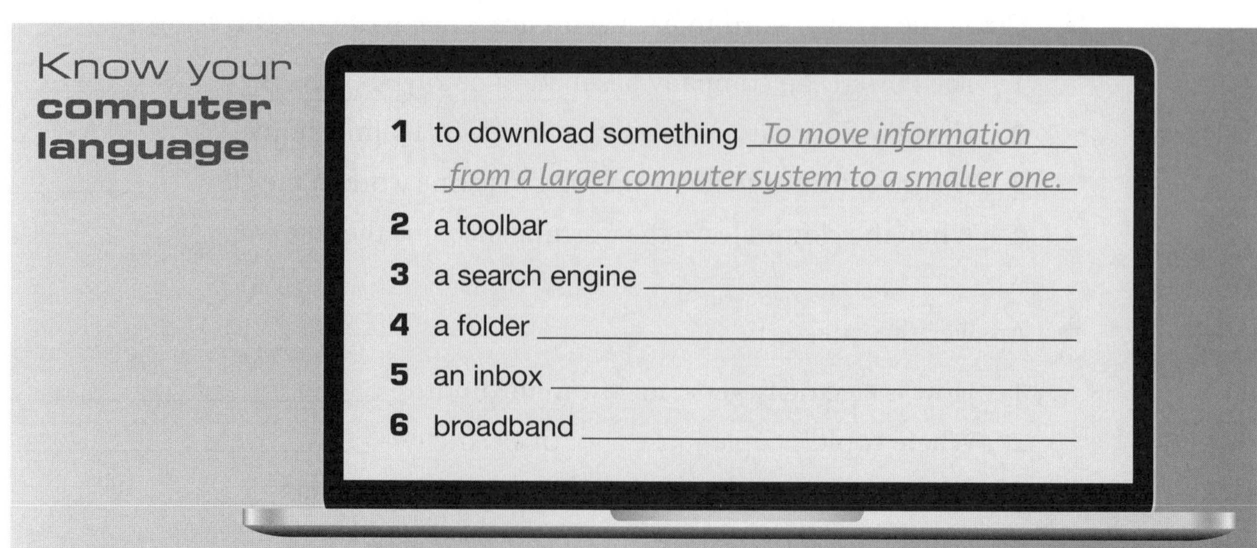

Know your **computer language**

1 to download something *To move information from a larger computer system to a smaller one.*
2 a toolbar ______
3 a search engine ______
4 a folder ______
5 an inbox ______
6 broadband ______

Reported speech

1 **Look at the picture. Then match the two halves of the sentences.**

1 The doctor said that _c_
2 The nurse said that ___
3 The boy said that ___
4 The little girl said that ___
5 The mother said that ___
6 The man said that ___

a cell phones weren't allowed.
b there was an apple in her bag.
c they didn't open until nine o'clock.
d his knee hurt.
e it was only a short message.
f she was hungry.

2 **Change the direct speech to reported speech. Remember that the pronouns need to change.**

1 Guan-Yu and Yu-Ting: "We don't have a good Internet connection."
Guan-Yu and Yu-Ting said that they didn't have a good Internet connection.

2 Minjun: "I'll quickly download those files."
____

3 Kanya and Sunisa: "We can find the link to that website."
____

4 Mia and Kate: "We're looking at the wrong menu."
____

5 Dang: "I'm moving the icons to a different place."
____

3 **Think of four things that people *said* or *told you* yesterday.**

My friend said that she was moving to a different school.

1 ______________________
2 ______________________
3 ______________________
4 ______________________

Reporting conversations

1 **Complete the phrases with the words in the box.**

about argument borrow heard said ~~sure~~ told

1 I'm _sure_ it'll be OK.
2 Did you hear ______ Mai and Kento?
3 I ______ they had an ______.
4 Mai ______ him that he could ______ her new tablet.
5 She ______ that he could use it for a day.

2 **Complete the conversation with the sentences from exercise 1.**

Jin Hi, Saki! [1] _Did you hear about Mai and Kento?_
Saki [2] ______ What was it about?
Jin Well, [3] ______.
Saki Really?
Jin Yes. [4] ______.
Saki That was nice of her.
Jin I know, but Kento deleted her favorite game!
Saki Oh, dear. I'm sure it was an accident.
Jin Yes, Kento told her that he would buy the game again and install it.
Saki Good. [5] ______ They're usually good friends.

3 **Write a conversation between you and a friend about a small argument.**

You Hi! Did you hear about ______?
Friend ______
You ______
Friend ______
You ______
Friend ______
You ______
Friend ______
You ______
Friend ______

Speech verbs

1 Choose the correct words.

1 "I broke your new camera," he **promised** / **admitted**.
2 "If you talk in the exam, you'll have to leave," the teacher **warned** / **giggled**.
3 "Excuse me, waiter! My plate is dirty," she **added** / **complained**.
4 "And the winner is – number 2!" the man **announced** / **insisted**.
5 "Don't make a noise or you'll wake the baby," she **agreed** / **whispered**.

2 Read the e-mail. What is Jane writing to Lisa about?

To: Lisa

Hi, Lisa

Hope everything is going well at school. Sorry I haven't written for ages – I've been really busy with exams.

Remember Dan and his sister, Emma? They moved away at the end of last year. They've made lots of new friends in their new town. Good to hear that they're happy. Dan told me last night that they wanted to come back and see us all. They're coming next weekend – probably early on Saturday afternoon.

I promised that I'd make dinner here on Saturday evening for them. Mom agreed that I could use the kitchen. You're invited, too. Want to come along a bit earlier and help?

Speak to you tomorrow. I'll give you a call you in the evening.

Love

Jane

3 Complete the sentences with one word from the text.

1 Jane has been busy with __________.
2 Last year, Dan and Emma moved to a different __________.
3 Dan and Emma are __________ where they live now.
4 Jane __________ her friends that she'd make a meal for them.
5 Jane would like Lisa to come and __________ her on Saturday.

4 Imagine that some friends moved away, but they are coming back to visit. Write an e-mail to another friend about it.

Write four paragraphs. Include the following information: 1) What you did recently; 2) Information about your friends; 3) Your plans for the visit; 4) When you will contact your friend.

Welcome

baht /bɑt/
dollar 🔑 /'dɑlər/
dong /dɑŋ/
kip /kɪp/
kyat /tʃæt/
peso /'peɪsoʊ/
renminbi /rɛnmɪn'bi/
riel /ri'ɛl/
ringgit /'rɪŋgət/
rupiah /ru'piə/
won /wɑn/
yen /yɛn/

Unit 1

babies 🔑 /'beɪbɪz/
belt 🔑 /bɛlt/
boots 🔑 /buts/
cap 🔑 /kæp/
children 🔑 /'tʃɪldrən/
connection 🔑 /kə'nɛkʃn/
dishonest 🔑 /dɪs'ɑnəst/
disorganized /dɪs'ɔrgə,naɪzd/
earrings /'ɪrɪŋz/
feet 🔑 /fit/
fishes 🔑 /'fɪʃɪz/
first impression /,fərst ɪm'prɛʃn/
frown /fraʊn/
high heels /,haɪ 'hils/
hoody /'hʊdi/
hoodies /'hʊdɪz/
impatient 🔑 /ɪm'peɪʃnt/
irresponsible /,ɪrɪ'spɑnsəbl/
leggings /'lɛgɪŋz/
lives 🔑 /laɪvz/
mice /maɪs/
patient 🔑 /'peɪʃnt/
people 🔑 /'pipl/
scarves /skɑrvz/
shelves 🔑 /ʃɛlvz/
sunglasses /'sʌn,glæsəz/
sweatpants /'swɛtpænts/
T-shirt /'ti ,ʃərt/
teeth /tiθ/
top 🔑 /tɑp/
unfashionable /ʌn'fæʃənəbl/
unkind 🔑 /ʌn'kaɪnd/
vest /vɛst/

Unit 2

bad-tempered /,bæd 'tɛmpərd/
cheerful /'tʃɪrfl/
dark-haired /'dɑrk ,hɛrd/
explanation 🔑 /,ɛksplə'neɪʃn/
generous 🔑 /'dʒɛnərəs/
kind-hearted /'kaɪnd ,hɑrtəd/
lazy 🔑 /'leɪzi/
left-handed /'lɛft ,hændəd/
may 🔑 /meɪ/
middle-aged /'mɪdl ,eɪdʒd/
might 🔑 /maɪt/
open-minded /'oʊpən ,maɪndəd/
organ donor /'ɔrgən ,doʊnər/
outgoing /'aʊt,goʊɪŋ/
receive 🔑 /rɪ'siv/
relaxed 🔑 /rɪ'lækst/
serious 🔑 /'sɪriəs/
short-sighted /,ʃɔrt'saɪt̬əd/
strange 🔑 /streɪndʒ/
talkative /'tɔkət̬ɪv/

Unit 3

ancient 🔑 /'eɪnʃənt/
apartment building /ə'pɑrt-mənt ,bɪldɪŋ/
awful 🔑 /'ɔfl/
boiling 🔑 /'bɔɪlɪŋ/
bridge 🔑 /brɪdʒ/
bungalow /'bʌŋgə,loʊ/
came 🔑 /keɪm/
can't wait to /'kænt ,weɪt tə/
desperately /'dɛsprətli/
earn money /,ərn 'mʌni/
enormous 🔑 /ɪ'nɔrməs/
excellent 🔑 /'ɛksələnt/
exhausted 🔑 /ɪg'zɔstəd/
factory 🔑 /'fæktəri/
farm 🔑 /fɑrm/
fascinating /'fæsə,neɪt̬ɪŋ/
field 🔑 /fild/
found 🔑 /faʊnd/
freezing 🔑 /'frizɪŋ/
furious 🔑 /'fyʊriəs/
gorgeous /'gɔrdʒəs/
highway 🔑 /'haɪweɪ/
hilarious /hɪ'lɛriəs/
hill 🔑 /hɪl/
lake 🔑 /leɪk/
midnight 🔑 /'mɪdnaɪt/
miserable /'mɪzrəbl/
missed 🔑 /mɪst/
parking garage /'pɑrkɪŋ gə,rɑʒ/
pulled down 🔑 /,pʊld 'daʊn/
river 🔑 /'rɪvər/
saw 🔑 /sɔ/
sidewalk /'saɪdwɔk/
starving /'stɑrvɪŋ/
terrifying /'tɛrə,faɪɪŋ/
thrilling /'θrɪlɪŋ/
village /'vɪlɪdʒ/
wonderful 🔑 /'wʌndərfl/
wood 🔑 /wʊd/

Unit 4

ankle 🔑 /'æŋkl/
blood 🔑 /blʌd/
bone 🔑 /boʊn/

🔑 a keyword of the **Oxford 3000** list showing words that are important and useful to learn.

/i/ **see**	/æ/ **cat**	/ʊ/ **put**	/ə/ **about**	/ɔɪ/ **boy**	/ər/ **bird**	/ɑr/ **car**
/ɪ/ **sit**	/ɑ/ **hot**	/u/ **too**	/eɪ/ **say**	/aʊ/ **now**	/ɪr/ **near**	/ɔr/ **door**
/ɛ/ **ten**	/ɔ/ **four**	/ʌ/ **cup**	/aɪ/ **five**	/oʊ/ **go**	/ɛr/ **hair**	/ʊr/ **tourist**

brain /breɪn/
a broken arm /ə ˌbroʊkən 'ɑrm/
a cold /ə 'koʊld/
calories /'kæləriz/
diet /'daɪət/
earache /'ɪreɪk/
exercise program /'ɛksərˌsaɪz ˌproʊgræm/
a fever /ə 'fivər/
follow /'fɑloʊ/
a headache /ə 'hɛdeɪk/
health /hɛlθ/
heart /hɑrt/
heart disease /'hɑrt dɪˌziz/
hip /hɪp/
kidneys /'kɪdniz/
knee /ni/
lifestyle /'laɪfstaɪl/
liver /'lɪvər/
lungs /lʌŋz/
muscles /'mʌslz/
nerves /nərvz/
shoulder /'ʃoʊldər/
skin /skɪn/
a sore throat /ə ˌsɔr 'θroʊt/
a sprained ankle /ə ˌspreɪnd 'æŋkl/
stomach ache /'stʌmək ˌeɪk/
throat /θroʊt/
tongue /tʌŋ/
unhealthy /ʌn'hɛlθi/
vegetarian /ˌvɛdʒə'tɛriən/
weight /weɪt/
wrist /rɪst/

Unit 5

chatroom /'tʃætrum/
classmate /'klæsmeɪt/
encourage /ɪn'kərɪdʒ/
especially /ɪ'spɛʃəli/
footlight /'fʊtlaɪt/
footwear /'fʊtwɛr/
furthermore /'fərðərˌmɔr/
get along with /ˌgɛt̬ ə'lɔŋ ˌwɪð/
get to know /ˌgɛt tə 'noʊ/
girlfriend /'gərlfrɛnd/
go out with your friends /ˌgoʊ ˌaʊt ˌwɪð yər ˌfrɛndz/
harmful /'hɑrmfl/
have a falling out with /ˌhæv ə ˌfɔlɪŋ 'aʊt ˌwɪð/
have a lot in common with /ˌhæv ə ˌlɑt̬ ɪn 'kɑmən ˌwɪð/
have an argument with /ˌhæv ən 'ɑrgyəmənt ˌwɪð/
headache /'hɛdeɪk/
incredibly /ɪn'krɛdəbli/
introduce somebody to /ˌɪntrə'dus ˌsʌmbədi tə/
laptop /'læptɑp/
make friends with /ˌmeɪk 'frɛndz ˌwɪð/
make up with /ˌmeɪk 'ʌp wɪð/
network /'nɛtwərk/
social life /'soʊʃl ˌlaɪf/
social network /ˌsoʊʃl 'nɛtwərk/
tennis /'tɛnɪs/
viewpoint /'vyupɔɪnt/
website /'wɛbsaɪt/
worldwide /ˌwərld'waɪd/

Unit 6

angry /'æŋgri/
arson /'ɑrsn/
arsonist /'ɑrsənɪst/
careful /'kɛrfl/
dangerous /'deɪndʒərəs/
dreadful /'drɛdfl/
famous /'feɪməs/
guilty /'gɪlti/
hack /hæk/
hacking /'hækɪŋ/
helpful /'hɛlpfl/
immediately /ɪ'midiətli/
knew /nu/
mug /mʌg/
mugger /'mʌgər/
mugging /'mʌgɪŋ/
murder /'mərdər/
mysterious /mɪ'stɪriəs/
national /'næʃənl/
natural /'nætʃrəl/
powerful /'paʊərfl/
robber /'rɑbər/
robbery /'rɑbəri/
set fire to /ˌsɛt 'faɪər tə/
shoplifting /'ʃɑpˌlɪftɪŋ/
speeding /'spidɪŋ/
theft /θɛft/
truthful /'truθfl/
unhelpful /ʌn'hɛlpfl/
vandal /'vændl/
vandalism /'vændlˌɪzəm/
vandalize /'vændlˌaɪz/

Unit 7

accountant /ə'kaʊntnt/
airport /'ɛrpɔrt/
apologize for /ə'pɑləˌdʒaɪz ˌfɔr, fər/
applicant /'æplɪkənt/
apply for /ə'plaɪ ˌfɔr, fər/
beauty salon /'byut̬i səˌlɑn/
beauty therapist /'byut̬i ˌθɛrəpɪst/
campaign /kæm'peɪn/
concentrate on /'kɑnsnˌtreɪt ˌɑn/

/p/ **pen**	/d/ **did**	/tʃ/ **beach**	/θ/ **thin**	/ʃ/ **she**	/m/ **man**	/r/ **red**
/b/ **bad**	/k/ **cat**	/dʒ/ **June**	/ð/ **then**	/ʒ/ **Asia**	/n/ **no**	/y/ **yes**
/t/ **tea**	/g/ **got**	/f/ **fall**	/s/ **so**	/h/ **how**	/ŋ/ **sing**	/w/ **wet**
/t̬/ **butter**		/v/ **very**	/z/ **zoo**		/l/ **leg**	

construction site /kənˈstrʌkʃn ˌsaɪt/
construction worker /kənˈstrʌkʃn ˌwərkər/
depend on /dɪˈpɛnd ˌɑn/
desk clerk /ˈdɛsk ˌklərk/
doorman /ˈdɔrmæn/
dream of /ˈdrim əv/
engineer /ˌɛndʒəˈnɪr/
firefighter /ˈfaɪərˌfaɪt̬ər/
fire station /ˈfaɪər ˌsteɪʃn/
impressive /ɪmˈprɛsɪv/
make somebody aware of /ˌmeɪk ˌsʌmˌbədi əˈwɛr əv/
nurse /nərs/
office worker /ˈɔfəs ˌwərkər/
pilot /ˈpaɪlət/
science lab /ˈsaɪəns ˌlæb/
scientist /ˈsaɪəntɪst/
successful /səkˈsɛsfl/
surgeon /ˈsərdʒən/
too good to be true /ˈtu ˌgʊd tə ˌbi ˈtru/
worry about /ˈwəri əˌbaʊt/

Unit 8

alarmed /əˈlɑrmd/
alarming /əˈlɑrmɪŋ/
amused /əˈmyuzd/
amusing /əˈmyuzɪŋ/
carbon dioxide /ˌkɑrbən daɪˈɑksaɪd/
catch a disease /ˌkætʃ ə dɪˈziz/
climate change /ˈklaɪmət ˌtʃeɪndʒ/
confused /kənˈfyuzd/
confusing /kənˈfyuzɪŋ/
depressed /dɪˈprɛst/
depressing /dɪˈprɛsɪŋ/
disappointed /ˌdɪsəˈpɔɪntəd/
disappointing /ˌdɪsəˈpɔɪntɪŋ/
effective /ɪˈfɛktɪv/
encouraged /ɪnˈkərɪdʒd/
encouraging /ɪnˈkərɪdʒɪŋ/
endangered species /ɪnˌdeɪndʒərd ˈspiʃiz/
fascinated /ˈfæsəˌneɪt̬əd/
fascinating /ˈfæsəˌneɪt̬ɪŋ/
fossil fuels /ˈfɑsl ˌfyuəlz/
frightened /ˈfraɪtnd/
frightening /ˈfraɪtnɪŋ/
global warming /ˌgloʊbl ˈwɔrmɪŋ/
irritated /ˈɪrəˌteɪt̬əd/
irritating /ˈɪrəˌteɪt̬ɪŋ/
known /noʊn/
mostly /ˈmoʊstli/
preventable /prɪˈvɛntəbl/
puzzled /ˈpʌzld/
puzzling /ˈpʌzlɪŋ/
raise money /ˌreɪz ˈmʌni/
renewable energy /rɪˈnuəbl ˌɛnərdʒi/
shocked /ʃɑkt/
shocking /ˈʃɑkɪŋ/
support /səˈpɔrt/
worried /ˈwərid/
worrying /ˈwəriɪŋ/

Unit 9

ask for a refund /ˌæsk fər ə ˈrifʌnd/
ATM /ˌeɪ ˌti ˈɛm/
borrow /ˈbɑroʊ/
cash /kæʃ/
cash register /ˈkæʃ ˌrɛdʒəstər/
change /tʃeɪndʒ/
cost /kɔst/
cost of living /ˌkɔst əv ˈlɪvɪŋ/
dip into your savings /ˌdɪp ˌɪntə yər ˈseɪvɪŋz/
figure out /ˌfɪgyər ˈaʊt/
free /fri/
healthcare /ˈhɛlθkɛr/
leisure /ˈliʒər, ˈlɛʒər/
lend /lɛnd/
mark down their prices /ˌmɑrk ˌdaʊn ðər ˈpraɪsɪz/
measure /ˈmɛʒər/
notice /ˈnoʊt̬əs/
owe /oʊ/
pay somebody back /ˌpeɪ ˌsʌmbədi ˈbæk/
PIN number /ˈpɪn ˌnʌmbər/
price /praɪs/
receipt /rɪˈsit/
reduced /rɪˈdust/
refund /ˈrifʌnd/
run out of money /ˌrʌn ˌaʊt̬ əv ˈmʌni/
sale /seɪl/
save up for a vacation /ˌseɪv ˌʌp fər ə veɪˈkeɪʃn/
shop around for the best prices /ˌʃɑp əˌraʊnd fər ðə ˌbɛst ˈpraɪsɪz/
take something back to the store /ˌteɪk ˌsʌmθɪŋ ˌbæk tə ðə ˈstɔr/

Unit 10

appetite /ˈæpəˌtaɪt/
astonishing /əˈstɑnɪʃɪŋ/
average /ˈævrɪdʒ/
beansprouts /ˈbinspraʊts/
beef /bif/
bell pepper /ˈbɛl ˌpɛpər/
bottle /ˈbɑt̬l/
bowl /boʊl/

/i/ see	/æ/ cat	/ʊ/ put	/ə/ about	/ɔɪ/ boy	/ər/ bird	/ɑr/ car
/ɪ/ sit	/ɑ/ hot	/u/ too	/eɪ/ say	/aʊ/ now	/ɪr/ near	/ɔr/ door
/ɛ/ ten	/ɔ/ four	/ʌ/ cup	/aɪ/ five	/oʊ/ go	/ɛr/ hair	/ʊr/ tourist

box /bɑks/
bread basket /'brɛd ˌbæskət/
carrots /'kærəts/
cheese /tʃiz/
chicken /'tʃɪkən/
chopsticks /'tʃɑpstɪk/
chunks /tʃʌŋks/
fewer /'fyuər/
flexible /'flɛksəbl/
glass /glæs/
gravy /'greɪvi/
green beans /ˌgrin 'binz/
involve /ɪn'vɑlv/
kebab /kə'bɑb/
mushrooms /'mʌʃrumz/
napkin /'næpkən/
noodles /'nudlz/
olives /'ɑlɪvz/
overweight /ˌoʊvər'weɪt/
package /'pækɪdʒ/
piece /pis/
placemat /'pleɪsmæt/
plate /pleɪt/
potatoes /pə'teɪt̬oʊz/
put on weight /ˌpʊt ˌɑn 'weɪt/
salt and pepper /ˌsɔlt ən 'pɛpər/
sauce dish /'sɔs ˌdɪʃ/
sausage /'sɔsɪdʒ/
scallions /'skælyənz/
side plate /'saɪd ˌpleɪt/
slice /slaɪs/
soup bowl /'sup ˌboʊl/
soup spoon /'sup ˌspun/
strong /strɔŋ/
tapas /'tɑpəs/
teacup /'tikʌp/
teapot /'tipɑt/
tomatoes /tə'meɪt̬oʊz/
tortilla /tɔr'tiyə/
towel /'taʊəl/

Unit 11

aluminum /ə'lumənəm/
apparently /ə'pɛrəntli/
bamboo /ˌbæm'bu/
brakes /breɪks/
brick /brɪk/
build /bɪld/
builder /'bɪldər/
building /'bɪldɪŋ/
button /'bʌtn/
china /'tʃaɪnə/
come up with /ˌkʌm 'ʌp ˌwɪð/
control panel /kən'troʊl ˌpænl/
design /dɪ'zaɪn/
designer /dɪ'zaɪnər/
develop /dɪ'vɛləp/
discover /dɪ'skʌvər/
discoverer /dɪ'skʌvərər/
discovery /dɪ'skʌvəri/
engine /'ɛndʒən/
exploration /ˌɛksplə'reɪʃn/
explore /ɪk'splɔr/
explorer /ɪk'splɔrər/
gears /gɪrz/
gold /goʊld/
handlebars /'hændlˌbɑrz/
invent /ɪn'vɛnt/
invention /ɪn'vɛnʃn/
inventor /ɪn'vɛntər/
leather /'lɛðər/
lever /'lɛvər, 'livər/
mechanism /'mɛkəˌnɪzəm/
nylon /'naɪlɑn/
pedal /'pɛdl/
plastic /'plæstɪk/
plenty of /'plɛnti əv/
powered by /'paʊərd ˌbaɪ/
propeller /prə'pɛlər/
rubber /'rʌbər/
silk /sɪlk/
steel /stil/
switch /swɪtʃ/
tailpipe /'teɪlpaɪp/
unusual /ʌn'yuʒuəl/
wheel /wil/
wool /wʊl/

Unit 12

add /æd/
admit /əd'mɪt/
agree /ə'gri/
announce /ə'naʊns/
argue /'ɑrgyu/
broadband /'brɔdbænd/
browser /'braʊzər/
clip /klɪp/
complain /kəm'pleɪn/
cursor /'kərsər/
document /'dɑkyəmənt/
engine /'ɛndʒən/
folder /'foʊldər/
giggle /'gɪgl/
icon /'aɪkɑn/
inbox /'ɪnbɑks/
insist /ɪn'sɪst/
link /lɪŋk/
menu /'mɛnyu/
promise /'prɑməs/
regret /rɪ'grɛt/
search /sərtʃ/
shout /ʃaʊt/
toolbar /'tulbɑr/
trash /træʃ/
warn /wɔrn/
whisper /'wɪspər/
window /'wɪndoʊ/

/p/ pen	/d/ did	/tʃ/ beach	/θ/ thin	/ʃ/ she	/m/ man	/r/ red
/b/ bad	/k/ cat	/dʒ/ June	/ð/ then	/ʒ/ Asia	/n/ no	/y/ yes
/t/ tea	/g/ got	/f/ fall	/s/ so	/h/ how	/ŋ/ sing	/w/ wet
/t̬/ butter		/v/ very	/z/ zoo		/l/ leg	

Conversation phrases

Unit 1 The look
Can I help you?
I'm looking for a sweater.
What about this one?
It's very nice, isn't it?
Do you have any other colors?
Can I try it on?

Unit 2 Characters
She's definitely the best player.
I don't think that ... .
In my opinion ... .
I think it's more important to ... .
Do you think so?

Unit 3 Places
Were you on vacation?
I was staying with my cousins.
Did you have a good time?
Was the weather good?
It was raining when we arrived.

Unit 4 Being human
What can I do for you today?
I'm not feeling very well.
What's the matter?
Do you have any other symptoms?
You have to drink plenty of water.
You should rest for a day or two.

Unit 5 Friends together
You're Sue, aren't you?
We've met before.
We met a couple of months ago.
I haven't seen Joe for a while.
Let me know next time.
Nice talking to you.
See you again soon.

Unit 6 Right or wrong?
I'd like to report a crime.
Can you describe what happened?
Where was this exactly?
Someone had broken the downstairs window.
Did you see anything / anyone suspicious?
Can you give me some more information?

Unit 7 Get to work!
India isn't as expensive as Britain.
That's such a good idea!
It's closer to home.
It's so expensive in the US.
The course doesn't take as long as the course here.

Unit 8 Fragile Earth
Do you have any plans for the weekend?
I'm going to make some posters.
Let's all meet at my house.
What time do you want to meet?
I'll call you later.
I'll wait to hear from you.

Unit 9 Money, money, money
Did you hear the news?
What happened?
Really? That's incredible!
You're kidding!
If that happened to me, I'd ... .

Unit 10 On the menu
Are you ready to order?
Could you tell me ... ?
What's that made with?
It's made with ... .
What would you like with that?
Any side orders or drinks?

Unit 11 Invention
Could you give me a hand, please?
What's the problem?
The remote control isn't working.
This is the button which ... .
When I press it, nothing happens.
There's a button which you press here.

Unit 12 Communicate
Did you hear about ... ?
I heard ... .
She told him that ... .
She said that ... .
I'm sure it'll be OK.